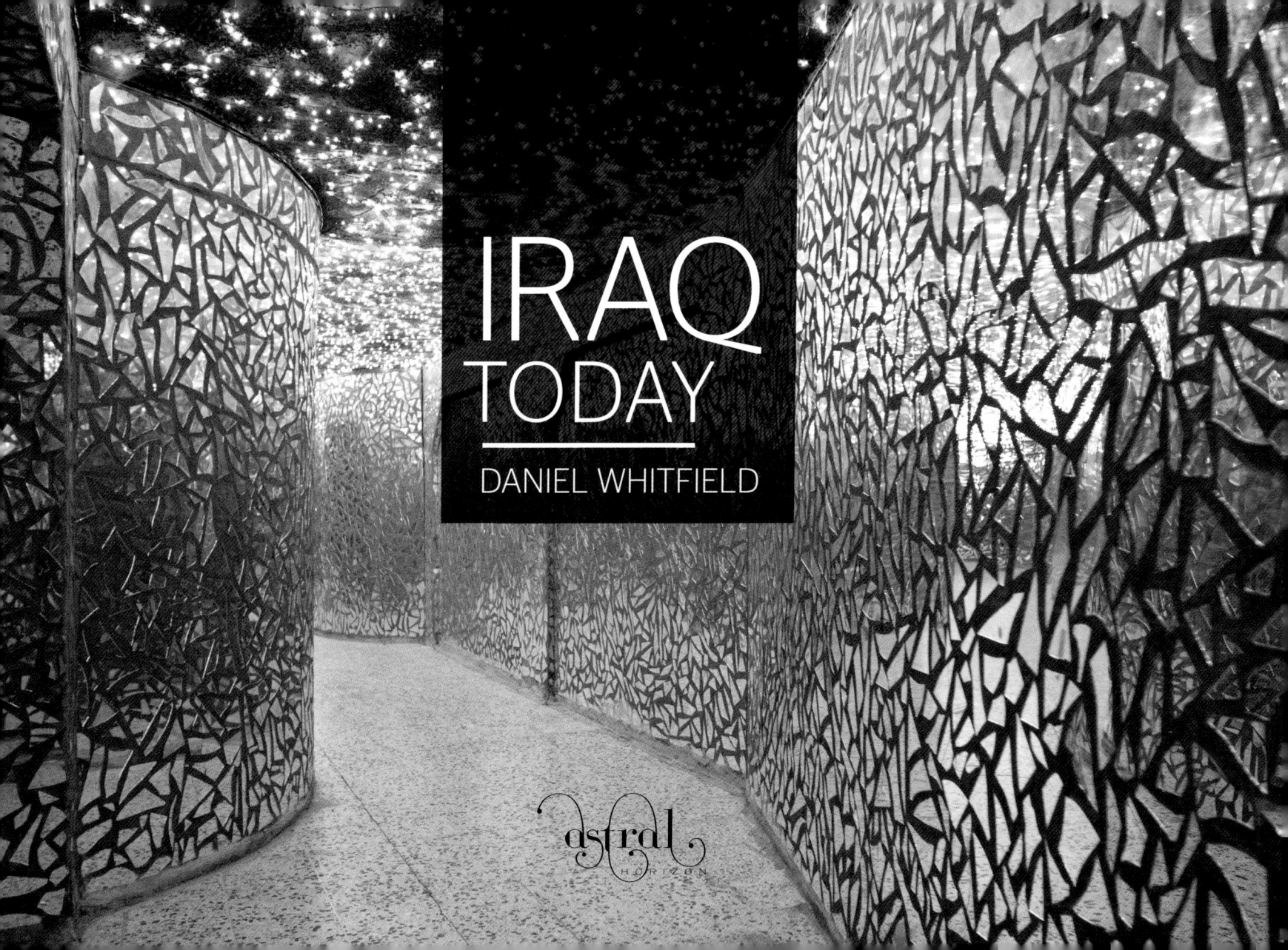

Astral Horizon Press
27 Meadow Road Claygate Surrey KT10 0RZ United Kingdom
www.theairlineboutique.com
ISBN 978-1-9160396-1-2

I would like to thank my guides Raad Al Qassimi, Sardar and Jan Ezidxelo on my three trips to Iraq. Their expert local knowledge and contacts were invaluable in experiencing and capturing the country up close and without incident. My eternal gratitude to Julian Nowill for the chance to see such an exceptional part of the Middle East. Also to my wife, Rianda, for her patience and support with my journeys away from home. My appreciation to Charles Kennedy and Astral Horizon Press for the opportunity to collate and share my photographs to a wider audience. Finally to the people of Iraq for their famous hospitality and genuine friendliness while visiting their historic and extraordinary country.

Iraq Today
Daniel Whitfield

Travels in Iraq with Daniel Whitfield, Raad Al Qassimi, Julian Nowill et fils, & Co.

by Charles Kennedy
editor and managing director, Astral Horizon Press

Iraq has dominated the headlines more than any other country for at least the last four decades – the drawn-out and failed invasion of neighbouring Iran was followed immediately by the disastrous adventure in Kuwait, resulting in a lost 1990s, mired under crippling sanctions. In 2003 the US invaded, unleashing a civil war which has taken the entire fifteen years since to play out.

Through all that, could civil society exist in any form? It was the human face of the country I was most curious to discover, and its ability to function after going through so much.

My first surprise was how little battle damage there is in Baghdad. During the 2003 invasion and initial occupation, there was urban fighting, but by the time US forces reached the capital, the first chapter of Iraq's war – the defeat of Saddam's government – had already been decided, and the city was taken without much of a struggle. The conflict that followed, against both occupation forces and rival Iraqi factions, claimed at least half a million lives nationwide, but even through that, the reality of violence in Baghdad was mostly car bombs, IEDs, suicide attacks. Such assymetrical warfare devasted lives, but left only a temporary mark on the surroundings, rather than the kind of street-to-street running battles that had chewed Beirut, and later, Syrian cities, down to rubble. Some Iraqi cities suffered that fate, as a cloud passes in front of the sun at the mention of Fallujah or Mosul.

What Baghdad is, is scruffy. Dear God is it scruffy. Decades without provision of even the most basic civic services – power, plumbing, rubbish collection – have left their mark. (In the post-Saddam era, Baghdad city officials contracted a Thai outfit to collect rubbish and sweep the streets, but with combat not yet over, they soon departed.) One of the untold stories of war is environmental destruction; the entire country carpeted is with plastic. And rampant construction without official permission or planning, both in the middle of the cities and also far out in the desert.

You might expect a recovering war zone to be abandoned, empty of life, derelict, especially with four million erstwhile citizens living outside the country. Not a bit of it. Baghdad is bursting at the seams with life. However shaky the economy might be, everywhere is brightly lit shops, showrooms, cafés, tailors, car repair workshops. Merchandise is piled high in the street and in busy covered markets.

It's a noisy city. The blare of traffic, the muezzine call to prayer, competing souk traders, Arabic scales and preachers' sermons from tinny speakers. And people everywhere. Iraq today is a nation of 40 million. Its growth, despite political travails, has been extraordinary. As recently as 1960 it was only 7.3 million, which is about the same as today's Baghdad, the Arab world's second-biggest city after Cairo.

Something I never expected was the degree to which the culture has survived. For sure the number of travel agencies in the cities attest to the number of people who left. Many have returned but an enormous Iraqi diaspora remains spread across the entire world – Houston, Montreal, Malmö, London, Berlin, Dubai, Jeddah, Sydney are just some of the cities with sizeable Iraqi expat communities. Our guide had sat out the worst of his country's convulsions as a reluctant guest of neighboring Syria, sitting in Aleppo unable to work, trying to live on savings as frugally as possible, returning on a shoestring as soon as it was safe, or safe enough. (Ironically, more recently, Syrians have sought shelter from their civil war in Iraq.)

Losing something along the way could happen. Indeed, Iraqis, more familiar with their travails and also with what they had before, may argue that something has been lost. If that is true, then the good news is how much they retained. There are book markets, art studios, record shops. We visited the Basra writers' guild, housed in a grand old Ottoman building, with an open central forum on two floors under an epic domed roof, the whole thing worn by a century or two of constant use. Next door was an exhibition of excellent work by the local art college's graduating class. Baghdad's famous Matanabbi Street book markets have editions in every language and on every subject. Down the end on the right is a literary café that has been home to intellectuals and dissidents for over a century, taking its name from the owner of the printing press that had been housed in the building, Abdel Majid Al-Shabander, hence Shabander's Café. Despite losing part of its collection to looters in post-invasion chaos, the National Museum of Iraq contains a staggeringly rich inheritance from the past, for all of humankind.

It gives a hint, with much evidence to follow, that the ancient civilisation of the Tigris and Euphrates is easily the equal of that of the Nile. Hot weather, lots of fresh water and lots of really good soil. Yet due to my overarching curiosity about contemporary society, I did not consider the archeological legacy that modern Iraq hovers over.

Salman Pak, notorious in the Saddam era for hosting a military facility which was the focus of the regime's 1980s biological and chemical weapons progammes, is home to Taq Kasra, a monument from the 3rd-6th century Sasanian-era, then part of ancient Persia, and the only visible structure remaining of the ancient city of Ctesiphon; today it is the largest single-span vault of unreinforced brickwork in the world and is considered a landmark in the history of architecture.

The remains of the ancient city of Babylon and its famous hanging gardens offer another overlap between the ancient world and the recent past, with one of Saddam's palaces on the hillside looking down on the historic ruins.

The Al-Ukhaidir Fortress, 50 kilometres south of Karbala, was built by a cousin of the Abbasid leadership in 775AD. Echoing halls, empty rooms, worn stone steps, iwans, courtyards. It is absolutely enormous. And there is nobody here, just the whistling of the wind.

The Sumarian ziggarat of Ur was part of a temple complex that served as the centre of the ancient city, and was a shrine to the moon god Nanna, and built by King Ur-Nammu in the 21st century BCE. With the passing of the centuries the ziggarat fell into disrepair, but was refurbished in the sixth century BCE by King Nabonidus, the last king of the Neo-Babylonian empire. With timelines like that, the past ceases to be old and almost becomes science fiction. In fact in southern Iraq, on the north shore of the point where the Euphrates and Tigris meet, is the site of the original, Biblical, literal Garden Of Eden.

The war is almost over. Even though factors such as uncertainty, corruption, climate change and a pariah reputation abroad still act as a handbrake to the future, the violence of the civil war and the struggle against ISIS have mostly been banished to the past. A new generation of young Iraqis are on their way up, waiting to inherit their ancient country, awash with culture, history, sunshine and human potential. Surely, after all their forebears have endured, this is a generation that will have a chance to enjoy it.

Charles Kennedy　　　　　　　　　　　　Claygate England, July 2019.

Looking down on wheat and barley farms irrigated from the Tigris River on the flight to Baghdad.

Disembarking at Baghdad International Airport, Iraq's largest airport and main hub for the state-owned Iraqi Airways.

A Iraqi Airways Boeing 727 on static display near Baghdad International Airport.

Migrating birds flying above the main carpark of Baghdad Airport

Mother and child on Bohan Street in Duhok, Iraqi Kurdistan.

Local residents shopping at Duhok Souq.

Afternoon tea in Duhok, served with copious sugar for local tastes.

Upmarket homes in Eastern Duhok, the capital of the Duhok Governorate in Iraqi Kurdistan.

Children on a residential rooftop in Duhok, Iraqi Kurdistan.

Syrian refugees in a makeshift camp on the outskirts of Duhok, Iraqi Kurdistan.

Baking flatbread at a restaurant in Baghdad.

The very grand and impressive main hall complete with elaborate chandolier and statue at Baghdad Central Station.

Blast walls and a watchtower outside the famous Hotel Palestine in Central Baghdad. Built in 1982 and originally operated by the French hotelier Le Méridien as the Palestine Méridien Hotel until UN sanctions were imposed following the first Gulf War.

Workers unloading boxes early Friday morning, Baghdad.

A monument in the city of Sulaymaniyah to Kurdish army officers who defected from the Iraqi army to the Kurdish resistance. When Saddam announced an amnesty they turned themselves in, only to be sent to Baghdad to be executed.

A poster outside of Iraqi Shia cleric, politician and militia leader, Muqtada al-Sadr.

Baghdad Central Station, designed and built by British architects and completed in 1953.

Signs above the ticket windows at Baghdad Central Station to the long ago discontinued destinations of Turkey and Syria. In its heyday services were also offered to Jerusalem and even as far west as London.

A Chinese CSR train that operates the country's only currently operational passenger route, from Baghdad to Basra.

The abandoned construction site of the Grand National Mosque. It was to be the largest mosque in the world but the 2003 US-led invasion halted its progress.

Gentlemen enjoying some morning tea in Sulaymaniyah, Iraqi Kurdistan.

A local merchant outside his shop, Sulaymaniyah, Iraqi Kurdistan.

The Bassetki Statue on display in the National Museum of Iraq in Baghdad. A monument from the Akkadian period (2350–2100 BCE) in Mesopotamia that was cast from pure copper and weighs 150 kilograms although only the lower part of the figure remains. It was looted from the museum during the 2003 invasion of Iraq but was recovered by American Military Police and found covered in axle grease and at the bottom of a cesspit after a tip-off.

Four Iraqi Kurds posing for a photo in Sulaymaniyah, Iraqi Kurdistan.

A picture of the Ishtar Gate, the eighth gate to the inner city of Babylon that was constructed in ~575 BC by order of King Nebuchadnezzar II. After excavation from 1902 to 1914 by the German Archaeologist, Robert Koldewey, the Ishtar Gate was rebuilt at the Pergamon Museum in Berlin in the 1930s.

The Grand Mosque of Sulaymaniyah, built by Prince Ibrahim Pasha Baban in 1784.

An Kurdish man in his workshop, Sulaymaniyah, Iraqi Kurdistan.

A busy street in the Shwaka neighbourhood of Baghdad.

Amna Suraka, or Red security prison. Under Saddam Hussein's regime the complex served as the northern headquarters of the Iraqi Intelligence Service, or the Mukhabarat.

An Iraqi family resting on the banks of the Tigris River, Baghdad.

A seller on Shuhada (Martyrs) Bridge, Central Baghdad.

A Saddam-era tank and military truck on display at Amna Suraka.

A couple crossing Shuhada (Martyrs) Bridge, Central Baghdad.

Men pushing a cart of boxes outside Mosque Wazzar, Central Baghdad.

Iraqi Policeman, Central Baghdad.

Names of female prisoners written on white bricks that were killed at Amna Suraka during the reign of Saddam Hussein.

The Hall of Mirrors, lined with 182,000 shards of mirrored glass, one for every victim of Saddam's Anfal campaign. The ceiling lights each represent one Kurdish village destroyed under Saddam.

Souk al-Safafeer in Central Baghdad. Originally a copper market but some of the shops have now been displaced by fabric shops.

Peshmerga guard, Sulaymaniyah, Iraqi Kurdistan.

Souk al-Safafeer is named after the arabic word for copper, "safra".

Shop owner at Souk al-Safafeer in Central Baghdad.

Plates of Iraqi leaders for sale at a shop in the souq. From left is Muqtada al-Sadr (the Iraqi Shia cleric), Masoud Barzani (former President of Iraqi Kurdistan), Saddam Hussein (no introduction needed), Abd al-Karim Qasim (an Iraqi Army brigadier who seized power in the 14 July Revolution in 1958 after the overthrow of the monarchy) and Mustafa Barzani (Kurdish nationalist leader).

Two Iraqi ladies, Souk al-Safafeer, Central Baghdad.

The busy Al Rasheed Street, one of the main streets in downtown Baghdad.

The town of Dokan surrounded by green hills, Sulaymaniyah Governorate, Iraqi Kurdistan.

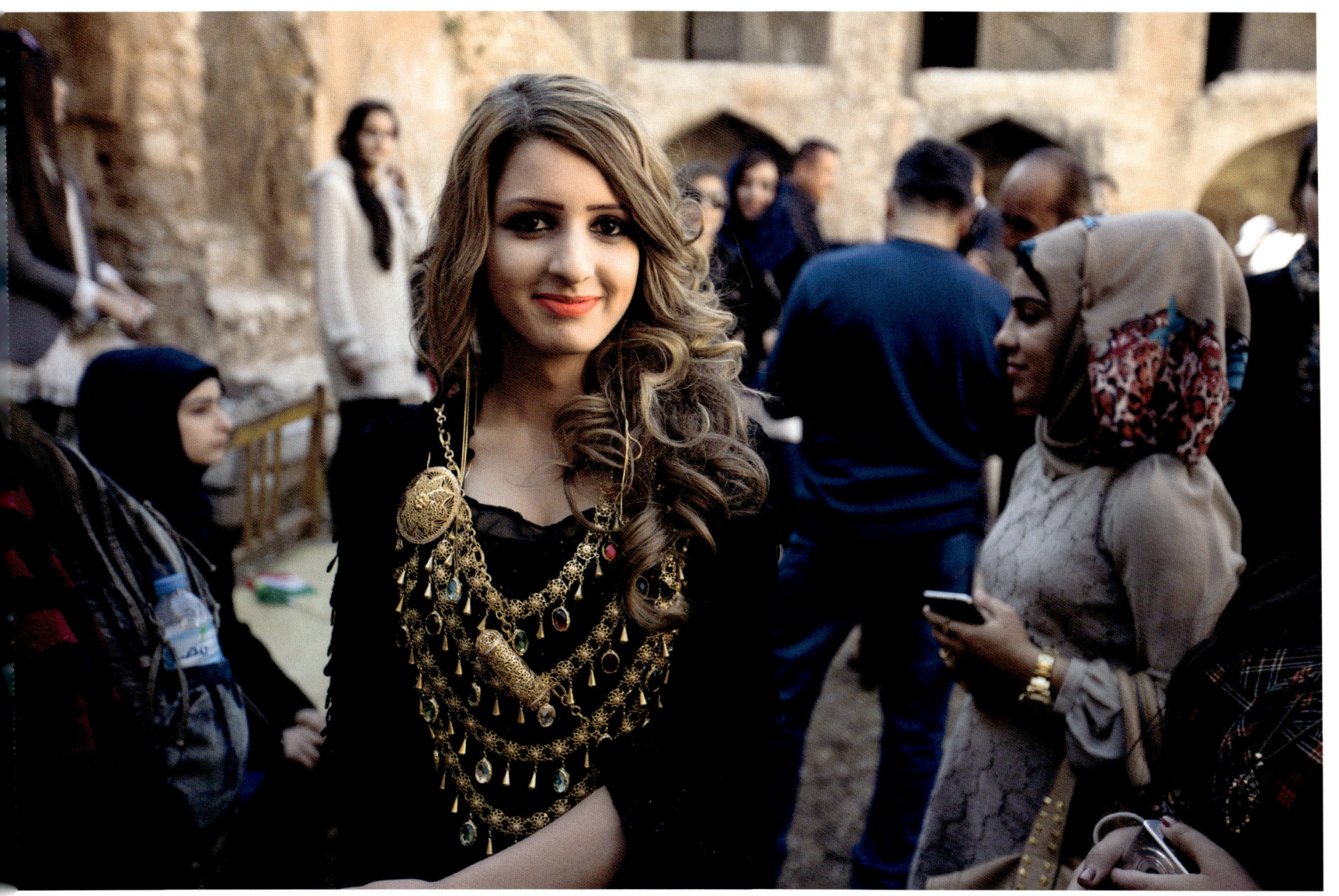
A college student visiting the old Koya caravanserai, an historic inn used for travellers and their horses to rest and recover.

An Arabic translation of the book "Debriefing The President" by John Nixon for sale on Mutanabbi Street, a street filled with bookstores and outdoor book stalls and named after the 10th-century classical Iraqi poet Al-Mutanabbi.

Shabandar Café, one of the most famous in Baghdad. The café was founded in 1917 in the building of a former printing press. The current owner (since 1963) is Haj Mohammed Al-Khashali.

A statue of the Iraqi poet Al-Mutanabbi at the end of Mutanabbi Street and on the banks of the Tigris river in Central Baghdad.

Cabinetmakers varnishing their handywork in Baghdad.

Tahrir (Liberation) Square, which commemorates the 1958 establishment of the Republic of Iraq and features a monument depicting the struggle of the Iraqi people to achieve liberty.

Armoured personnel carriers blocking the road in Baghdad. There are frequent government protests on Friday morning in the city after prayers so the Police close some of the roads to traffic to allow the people to march unimpeded.

The unfinished Al-Rahman mosque in Baghdad's Mansour neighbourhood, another mosque that was halted after the 2003 invasion.

Father and son at a street side sweet stall in Erbil, Iraqi Kurdistan.

Students enjoying a picnic, Koye, Iraqi Kurdistan.

Erbil's Jalil Khayat Mosque, modelled on the Blue Mosque in Istanbul.

The Citadel in Erbil, currently under restoration by UNESCO and the KRG, has been on the World Heritage List since June 2014.

Row of stalls and crowds of shooped at the Erbil souq.

Boys in the back of pickup at a service station, north of Baghdad.

One of the many checkpoints on the road north of Baghdad. Although the checkpoints just outside Baghdad were manned by the Iraqi Police, further north they are under the control of the Shi'ite Militia led by Muqtada al-Sadr.

The Malwiya Minerette, Samarra.

Iraqis climbing the spiralling steps of the Malwiya Minaret.

Looking down on the remains of the Great Mosque of Samarra from the top of Malwiya Minaret.

A spy surveillance balloon tethered above a military base, Baghdad.

Diners at a restaurant in the town of Salman Pak, Baghdad Governate.

A mother and son in the main street beside an Iraqi Army Humvee in Salman Pak, Baghdad Governate.

Pilgirms at Al Sahaabi Salman Al Farsi Shrine, Salman Pak, Baghdad Governate.

A panorama of the ruins of Taq Kasra, often referred to as the Archway of Ctesiphon.

Ctesiphon was an ancient city located on the eastern bank of Tigris. The archway is the last remaining structure and was once a part of the royal palace in Ctesiphon and is estimated to date between the 3rd and 6th centuries AD.

The late afternoon sun shining through the arch, which is also the largest single-span vault of unreinforced brickwork in the world.

The Ctesiphon visitor centre, Salman Pak, Baghdad Governate.

Looking down on the ruined pool, recreation area and snack bars of the visitor centre.

Al Sahaabi Salman Al Farsi Shrine at dusk in Salman Pak, Baghdad Governate.

Some of the original brickwork under restoration and maintenance of the Palace of Nebuchadnezzar II (king of Babylon from 605 BC to 562 BC).

When Saddam toured the reconstruction and when he asked the curators how they knew when the original palace was built, they showed him one of the original bricks stamped with the name of King Nebuchadnezzar II and the construction date, 605 BC.

The Iraqi leader then immediately suggested that the bricks used in the recreation bear a similar inscription. Hence they are inscribed with the text: "In the reign of the victorious Saddam Hussein, the president of the Republic, may God keep him, the guardian of the great Iraq and the renovator of its renaissance and the builder of its great civilization, the rebuilding of the great city of Babylon was done in 1987".

In 1983 Saddam Hussein ordered the rebuilding of Babylon. As most Iraqi men were fighting in the bloody Iran-Iraq war, Saddam brought in thousands of Sudanese workers to lay brand new yellow bricks over where the Palace of Nebuchadnezzar II (king of Babylon from 605 BC to 562 BC) had stood.

A group of visiting Iraqi's visiting the reconstructed Palace. Saddam's perhaps misguided attempt to reconstruct the Palace of Nebuchadnezzar II has been derided as 'Disney for a Despot' as it was violating the archaeological principle of preserving rather than recreating.

Looking over to the former Summer Palace of Saddam Husseim with the original ruins of Babylon in the foreground. Following the 2003 American invasion, US camp Alpha was set up partially on the ruins. Significant damage occurred with areas leveled to create landing pads for helicopters and parking lots for vehicles, tanks rumbled over ancient bricks, Polish troops dug trenches through a ancient temple and soil holding artifacts and bones was scooped into sandbags.

Wooden date palms adorning the wall in the Palace lobby.

A man taking a photo of his daughter in what appeared to be a larger living room.

Despite being almost 15 years since the fall of Saddam, Iraqis still visit the former palace with the fascination and inquisitiveness.

Selling tea in the city of Hillah.

Situated ~50 kilometres west of the city of Karbala, Al-Ukhaidir Fortress was constructed during the 8th century and was an important stop on regional trade routes.

The high perimeter walls of the fort built for defence and are also a very interesting and elegant example of early Islamic architecture. Since 2000 the fortress has been on the tentative UNESCO World Heritage list.

Night street scene, Karbala.

A shop selling fresh popcorn in the city of Karbala, Southern Iraq.

Outside the Al Abbas Mosque, which is the home of the tomb of Abbas ibn Ali, the son of Imam Ali (cousin and son-in-law of Muhammad), the first Imam of Shia Muslims and the fourth Caliph of Sunni Muslims.

Outside the Shrine of Imam Husayn ibn Ali, the mosque and burial site of the third Imam of Islam and is located near where he was martyred during the Battle of Karbala in 680 AD.

Families enjoying the cool evening temperature with the Shrine of Imam Husayn ibn Ali in the distance.

Sweets for sale in Karbala, Southern Iraq.

Ladies being taxiied about on a cart in the city of Karbala, Southern Iraq.

A seemingly endless row of faces of soldiers killed in the fight against ISIS on the side of the road east of Karbala.

Inside Al-Nukhailah Mosque in Al Kifl. It is also the site of tomb of the Islamic Prophet Dhul-Kifl, mentioned twice in the Koran and who is often identified as Ezekiel, a Hebrew prophet who preached to the Jews in captivity under Nebuchadnezzar in the sixth century BC.

Hebrew writing at the tomb of the Islamic Prophet Dhul-Kifl.

Up until 1947 there was an Iraqi Jewish population of ~156,000 and was one of the largest and most prominent Jewish communities in the Middle East. Until the mid-20th century, over 5,000 Jewish pilgrims used to come to the tomb all over Iraq during Passover. Following the creation of Israel in 1948, the entire Jewish population had no choice but to leave, with only 10 remaining today.

An Iraqi man enjoying tea at the Ottoman-era Al Kifl souq.

A busy street in the city of Najaf.

Khubz Shakar Al Ghadir (bread of thanksgiving) in Najaf, Southern Iraq.

A fruit vendor in an open street market in the city of Najaf.

An Iraqi lady dressed in a head-to-toe black chador in Najaf.

The setting sun on the main street in Najaf.

Ladies posing for a photo in Najaf.

The long and bustling souq in Najaf.

Outside the main entrance to Imam Ali Mosque. The mosque is home to the tomb of Imam Ali, the cousin of Muhammad, the first Imam (according to Shia belief) and fourth caliph (according to Sunni belief).

Biscuits and sweets for sale in Najaf souq.

Women wearing the chador in Karbala, Southern Iraq.

Sweet basbousa for sale in Najaf souq.

Brassware in Najaf souq.

Men shopping for suit fabric at Najaf souq.

An abandoned military outpost beside the road, left over from the time of the US occupation, east of Najaf.

Fresh fruit and vegetables for sale on the highway between Najaf and Afak.

A pump at a service station dispensing petrol for $0.38 per litre ($1.44 per US gallon).

At the archaeological site of Nippur. Also visiting are Iraqis out on a cultural excursion.

Nippur was first briefly excavated in 1851 before being more thoroughly between 1889 and 1900 by archaeologists from the University of Pennsylvania. This brick structure had been built by the American archaeologists on top of the old temple ruins around 1900.

A pool hall in the town of Afak.

The Great Ziggurat of Ur. The Ziggurat was built originally during the early Bronze Age period (21st century BC) and then restored in 6th century BC by King Nabonidus. During the reign of Saddam Hussein the façade of the lowest level and the monumental staircase were restored and rebuilt.

Looking south to the ruins of Ur, believed to be the birthplace of Abraham, and to Ali Air Base in the distance.

Robotic Santas outside a restaurant in the city of Nasiriyah.

Cattle grazing at the lush and green Mesopotamian Marshes.

At a small roadside stall beside the marshes. The inhabitants of the Tigris-Euphrates marshlands are the Marsh Arabs.

A boy in a mashoof canoe in the marshes.

A simple pole is the more traditional means of propelling the narrow boats through the reed and water.

An Iraqi teenager aboard a boat at the confluence of the Tigris (right) and Euphrates (left) rivers where they meet to form the Shatt al-Arab before continuing on to the Persian Gulf.

A couple crossing the street beside an Iraqi Army Hummvee in the city of Basra, Southern Iraq.

Colourful stained glass windows in an old Ottoman era building, occupied by the Basra Writers' Guild.

Girls arriving at a school in Basra Old Town.

Contemporary art by Iraqi artists at a gallery in Basra.

Imam Ali Mosque, Basra. The present day mosque sits at the site of the Old Mosque of Basra, the first to be built in Iraq following the Arab conquest in 636 AD. Only part of the minaret remains from the original mosque however.

Copies of the Holy Quran at Imam Ali Mosque, Basra.

Basra Sports City Stadium. After construction began in July 2009 it was completed four years later in October 2013.

The stadium is the home of the Iraq national football team and held its first international match with a friendly against Jordan in June 2017, with Iraq winning 1-0.

Yellow Iranian-made taxis in the centre of Basra, Southern Iraq.

Clothing stalls cluttering a canal bridge in central Basra, Southern Iraq.

An arms shop in Basra Souq.

A man sitting on a bridge over a canal in the city of Basra, Southern Iraq.

A recently constructed Italian designed suspension bridge over the Shatt al-Arab that opened for its first traffic in August 2017.

The former Saddam Hussein Presidential Palaces Compound on the Shatt al-Arab in Basra, Southern Iraq.

A family leaving the colourful Basra fairground.